Steve Urkel's

☆

Super-Cool

Guide
to
Success

Steve Urkel's

☆

Super-Cool
Guide to Success

Humorous Urkel tips
on how to win at . . .
fashion, finance, romance,
and more!

Special thanks to: Jean Feiwel, Bernette Ford, Sonia Black, Veronica Ambrose, Karen McTier, Sheryl Haft, Patricia Brown, Jennifer Bunda, Kelly Lindsey, Michelle Sucillon, Laurie Pessell, and Carole Franklin.

Produced by Creative Media Applications
Written by Billy Aronson
Art Direction by Fabia Wargin Design

To my "Laura," Lisa

ISBN 0-590-45744-6

12 11 10 9 8 7 6 5 4 3 2 1   2 3 4 5 6 7 / 9

Printed in the USA   40

First Scholastic printing, August 1992

Table of Contents

Introduction *1*

How to Succeed at Romance *3*

Choosing Your Suspenders *7*

How to Succeed at Your Job *9*

How to Succeed at Hand-to-Hand Combat *11*

Breaking into Song *13*

How to Kiss *16*

Laughing for Success *18*

How to Succeed on the Dance Floor *20*

How I Got to be So Cool *22*

Finding Your Own "Did I Do That?" *23*

Foreign Languages *26*

How to be Included When People Forget to Invite You .. *28*

How to Protect Your Locker *30*

Defending Your Honor *31*

How to Build Your Own Laboratory *33*

Shakespeare and You *35*

How to Succeed in Gym *38*

On Being Different *40*

The Importance of the Cord Attached to My Glasses *42*

Urkel Style *43*

Eyebrow Power *44*

Quick Wit *45*

Investing for Success *46*

Getting the Teacher to Call on You *49*

Writing the Love Poem *50*

Farewell *52*

Final Urk-Zam *53*

Hey there, young
reader! It's me, your
old pal Steve Urkel,
here to congratulate
you on your choice of
reading material. The
book you now hold in
your hands will help you
open doors. It will help
you move mountains. It
will help you reach
your dreams and
impress your
friends. That's
right, this book
holds the secrets to
success. Be all you
can be: **Read it.**

Can this book bring
anybody success? No, not just
anybody. For the book to work,

you've got to be a little bit special. But I know you're special. How? Because out of all the books in the store —books by famous athletes, rock stars, and the greatest writers of all time — you chose a book from Steven Q. Urkel. **Yep, you're special all right.**

Some of you don't believe a super successful guy like me would really tell his secrets. You're wrong. I'm spillin' the beans. I'm giving the inside scoop — and more. I'm giving the inside shovelful.

I've decided to spill my precious secrets to success for three reasons. First, because I have a burning desire to share my wisdom. Second, because I long to help dreamers, underdogs, and good kids everywhere. Third, because I need the cash. That's right, I'm saving up to have a life-sized bronze statue of Laura built on the front lawn at school. (Just imagine the look on her face when she beholds it, glimmering in the sunlight for everyone to see. Her feelings for me will be even stronger than they are now.)

So to all my fans who are reading this book, you may now begin your march on the golden road to glory, greatness, and success.

How to Succeed at
Romance

Some people say love makes the world go round. It definitely makes the Urkel go round! I think about my true love 24 hours a day, 7 days a week, and on holidays, too. She's the apple of my eye, the music of my ear, the rose of my nose, the sock on my toes, the sun in my sky, the cream in my cocoa, and the "ee eye ee eye" in my "ee eye ee eye oh."

For those of you who may not know who she is (Where've you been, on the moon?!), her name is Laura.

The apple of *your* eye may have some other name, like Marilyn, Nancy, Harvey, or Mister Chimp. But in this book I'll call your special someone your "Laura" because this will keep things simple — and because just typing her name gives me the tingles. *Laura Laura* — ooo! — *Laura Laura Laura* — my fingertips are buzzing with delight! *Laura Laura Laura Laura Laura Laura* — uh oh — *Laura Laura Laura Laura* — I'm losing control — *Laura Laura Laura Laura* — my fingertips are going wild! *Laura Laura Laura Laura* — Please don't put down the book, reader — *Laura Laura* — I'll have my fingertips back under control in just one little second — *Laura Laura Laura Laura Laura Laura*. Whew, that was fun!

The so-called experts will tell you that the best way to win your Laura's heart is by playing it cool. They'll say that "absence makes the heart grow fonder," so you should wait for your Laura to come to you.

Hogwash!

Your Laura is a heavenly creature, a perfect angel, right? Waiting for somebody like that to come to you would be like waiting for Halley's comet.

That's why the Urkel plan for winning your Laura is much more direct: **Give it all ya got, amigo.** Smother your Laura with kindness in every way you can think of. Carry her books. Bring her flowers. Write her letters. Play her love songs on your accordion. (If you don't have an accordion, any extremely loud musical instrument will do.)

Always be there for her. Be there to pick up anything she drops. Be there to clean up anything she spills. Be there to help her up when she trips. (Whenever possible, you should try not to be the *cause* of all the dropping, spilling, and tripping!)

Become interested in anything she's interested in. Love what she loves, hate what she hates, and be wishy-washy about things she's wishy-washy about. If she finds something sad, you should break into tears. If she makes a joke, laugh your head off.

To prove your love you must be willing to get down on your hands and knees and worship the very ground your Laura walks on! (This can really hurt if she's wearing cleats.)

At first your Laura might seem puzzled by all this kindness. She might look a little scared or confused, or like she's about to faint.

But don't be fooled, true lover. Your Laura is just playing hard to get, the shy little thing. Do not let up with your shower of kindness. **Shower away!**

Your Laura might keep on playing hard to get. In fact, she might play even harder to get. Then she might play harder and harder to get, and then incredibly hard to get. Then she might play impossible to get.

But one thing's for sure: She'll definitely know who you are. Your Laura will never forget you, love warrior. You'll have won a lasting place in her mind, her heart, and her dreams (although one or two of those dreams might be nightmares).

Suspenders

The road to success is full of bumps. So when you're out there laboring for your Laura, every now and then you're bound to stumble, trip, or walk into a wall. You can make it through the rough and tumble action with your pride unharmed as long as you're sure of one thing: **Your pants must not fall down**. That's why suspenders are a must.

Suspenders give people a good feeling about you. They give everyone a feeling of old-fashioned honesty and charm. Plus, they hold your pants up.

The main thing to think about when choosing suspenders is the color. You want bright. You want bold. You want suspenders that cry out across a crowded room, "We're suspenders!" Red is my favorite color for suspenders, followed by yellow, purple, green, and glow-in-the-dark orange.

The other thing to consider is stretchiness. Suspenders that are way too loose are a drag — they *drag* behind you everywhere you go. Little dogs get all tangled up in them. Suspenders that are too tight can also cause trouble. When you raise your hand in class they come flying off and wrap around the flag. Then the whole class has to pledge allegiance to your suspenders.

So spend as much money as you must, to get the suspenders that are just right for you. Be a big suspender spender!

Your Job

There are only three reasons I can think of to get a job: to make money so you can shower your Laura with gifts, to make money so you can take your Laura to a movie, or to be near your Laura while *she's* working. In each case, there's a lot on the line. You can't come in late, Nate. You can't clown around, Jimmy Brown. You can't just do what you wanna, Winona. You've gotta do well, Raphael!

Every time I start a new job the boss gives me the same old tired advice: "Just do what you can." Just do what I can? Me? Steven Q. Urkel — the Wurkel-holic?! It'll be a cold day in July when I *just* do what I can!

So I've adjusted the "Just do what you can" rule slightly. My advice for on-the-job success is: **"Just do <u>more</u> than you possibly can."** If you're shoveling snow with one shovel, slide another shovel under your chin and shovel double! If you're carrying two grocery bags in your arms, put another one between your legs and deliver double! If you're carrying dirty dishes in your hands, balance some more plates on your shoulders, on your forehead, on your nose...

Sure, every now and then this extra effort may lead to a little spill. Or a small collision. Or some spaghetti on the floor and meatballs on a chair and french fries on a window and chili dogs on the counter and cheesecake on the door and a hot fudge sundae with whipped cream and nuts dripping from the ceiling... but hey! Customers who said you were "just another worker" will have to eat their words (even if they won't be able to eat their meal).

How to Succeed in
Hand-to-Hand
Combat

I wish there were no need for this chapter. **Wouldn't it be nice if we all could live in peace and harmony?** Or even just peace and out-of-tune singing! But there are Fuffners out there. There are vicious villains, nasty no-goodniks, and evil-doing evildoers. These brutal bullies will stop at nothing to stop *you* on the way to success.

They may make trouble for your Laura, or your friends, or you. If you stand up to the bullies

— and you should — there's a chance you'll have to defend yourself in hand-to-hand combat.

But do not fear, reader dear, the Marquis of Urkelsberry's rules are here! These two simple rules will help you beat the bully before he beats you.

Rule number one is: **Study.** Study every book you can find on every kind of fighting. Study all the secrets of boxing, wrestling, judo, tae kwon do, and wai no no (the ancient art of tickling).

Can studying make you safe against a towering bully's 200 pounds of solid muscle? No way. That's why you'll also need rule number two: **Move very quickly.** When facing the bully you've gotta run circles around him. You've gotta dodge, dart, leap, scamper, scurry, skip, spin, flip, flit, and dance the love duet from *Swan Lake*. Dance around the clod till he's dizzy.

How come a little swiftness can totally daze a bully? Because of a very important fact about bullies I've learned from my years of dealing with bullies of every scary shape and size: They're out of touch!

Breaking into
Song

Hold onto your seats, Urkel fans. I'm about to give you a tip that's almost too hot to type. Whenever you really need to impress people with your coolness, break into s—*youch!* I told you the tip was hot. I burnt my fingers! Break into so— *oo ee ow ouch.* **Break into song!**

Have you ever heard me break into my rap "Do the Urkel" at a party? I'm sure you've heard me go into a verse of "Camptown Races" ("Doo dah, doo dah") many a time. When I sing — people notice!

You can do it, too. Just take your favorite song and change the words to make them right for you. I wrote the words to a hit song that I'm waiting to use on Laura at just the right moment. I call it "Justify My Laugh."

Here's a song I wrote for another special occasion to the tune of "The Star Spangled Banner":

The Star Spangled Urkel
by Francis S. Key & Steven Q. Urkel

Oh say, can you hear
My accordion all right?
That so loudly I played
While the Winslows were snoring

With my glasses so large
And suspenders so bright
Whether yellow or red
Well,they never are boring

And my laugh, did you hear?
Did I snort in your ear?
That tells you, my dear
That your Urkel is here!

Oh say, does that Steve Urkel yet rule?
He's the prince of the swift
And the king of the cool!

I'm hoping to sing that before the first game
of the World Series. Although any nationally
televised event would be fine.

But enough about me! Here's a song for you
to sing to your Laura, to the tune of "Camptown

Races." Save this song for one of those special moments when you've knocked over half the stuff in her house. I wrote most of it. You just have to fill in the blanks.

Song For _____
        (Fill in the name of your Laura)
by Steven Q. Urkel &
_____ __. _____ (your name)

I spilled _____ all over you
Doo dah, doo dah
Broke your father's _____ too
Oh the doo dah day
Bent your _____ a bit
But don't have a fit!
Cause, _____, my love is true
Oh the doo dah day!!

With songs like this one you're sure to bring down the house. If you haven't brought down the house already!

How to
Kiss

Every lesson you've read so far in this book has been based on years of thinking and testing. This lesson is based on years of thinking, but unfortunately, very little actual testing!

When it comes to kissing, I don't have a ton of experience. But I have done a lot of reading, planning, and practicing on a cantaloupe. You can be sure I'll be ready when Laura finally breaks down and says, "Okay, Steve baby, plant one right here."

The key to a kiss, I believe, is in the pucker. People who are too shy hardly pucker at all. I'm gonna go for a big proud pucker. **The prouder the pucker the purer the passion.**

Once you've got your pucker in place, move your face right in towards your Laura's face. Zoom those lips straight in for the kill... like deadly dive bombers.

Then comes the moment you've been waiting for: the big smoocheroo. Press those babies against her waiting lips and smack 'em with all you've got.

I've practiced these steps so many times that my cantaloupe is mildewed. How clearly I can picture it! My lips pucker. Her lips pucker. My face moves towards hers. Her face moves towards mine. I leap onto her lap. She falls off the couch. I pull her back up. The coffee table flips over. A bookshelf tumbles to the ground. A fuse box explodes. Sparks fly all around. Fire fighters come rushing in with hoses and axes and barking dalmatians that jump all over the furniture...

Yep, I just know when I finally kiss Laura it'll be a moment neither of us will ever forget!

Laughing for
Success

Let's face it: **My laugh sets me apart.** There can be a hundred people laughing in a crowd, but when my snort kicks in everybody looks!

This snort o' success comes naturally to me. But even if you're cursed with a boring, everyday laugh, **you too can get yourself a laugh that will set you apart.**

So kiss your humdrum HA HA goodbye. Leave your plain old TEE HEE behind. Make up a laugh that will really be worth laughing.

One idea is to build on your natural chuckle.

After the HA HA HA, throw in a sneeze, a cough, or a loud hiccup. Or you could start hooting like an owl. Or howling like a hyena. Or crowing like a rooster. Imagine that one — HA HA HA COCK-A-DOODLE-DOOOOOOO. Now there's a laugh people would notice.

Or try giving your laugh a tune. Imagine a laugh to the tune of Beethoven's *Fifth Symphony:*
HA HA HA *HAAAAAAA!*
HA HA HA *HAAAAAAA!* HA HA HA *HAAA,* HA HA HA *HAAA,* HA HA HA *HAAAAA!* HA HA HA *HAAA,* HA HA HA *HAAA,* HA HA HA *HAAAAA!*
HA HA HA *HAAAAAAAAA!* HA HA HA *HAAAAAAAAA!* HA HA HA *HAAAA —HAAAA — HAAAAAAAAAAAAAAAAAAAAA AAAAAAAA!*

This laugh would be perfect if you like to laugh for a long time. The symphony goes on for almost an hour!

Whatever laugh you choose, the important thing is to be brave. Don't just sit there alone in your room, laughing to yourself. Get out there! Laugh and let laugh. People may laugh at your laugh. But at least they'll notice your laugh. So let the laughers laugh. **He who laughs last, laughs best!**

How to Succeed on the
Dance Floor

The two coolest moves ever danced on any floor are: the Michael Jackson Moonwalk and the Urkel Shuffle. Of course, you'll never find yourself out on the dance floor moving like me. That's the bad news. But you can still strut your stuff with style.

Here's the secret to cool dancing in three words: **Be yourself.** (Uh oh! I should have said, "Here's the secret to cool dancing in *two* words, one of which has two syllables: Be yourself." Hooray for parentheses!)

So when you get out on the dance floor, be yourself. If you're wiry like me, twist your limber limbs in a million different ways. If you're seven feet tall and have enormous feet, let those feet do some serious stomping. (Just make sure they don't stomp on us little wiry guys.)

Whatever your size or shape, **let loose.** You have nothing to be ashamed of but shame itself. If you remember to be yourself, you're sure to set the dance floor on fire — without burning it down!

How I Got to be
So Cool

At this point you're probably asking yourself, "Steven Q. Urkel? How *did* you get to be so cool?"

I wish I could explain it. **As far back as I can remember, I've had that certain something.**

Right from the first I was a step ahead of the other kids. When they were just learning to crawl, I was already tripping over things.

I started speaking when I was only eight months old. One day when Mom was changing my diaper, I looked up at her and said in my sweet little voice, "Did I do that?" I'd never seen a grown woman faint before.

Why, I can still remember the first time I snorted as if it were yesterday. I was lying in my crib and Dad reached in to tickle me. But instead of the little giggle he was expecting, I let out a high-pitched snort. I'd never seen a grown man scream before.

I guess what I'm saying is: You can learn coolness, you can win success, but you've gotta be born Urkel.

Finding Your Own
"Did I Do That?"

Doesn't it seem like everything's always falling over nowadays? They must not put much care into making sturdy furniture. Or pottery. Or people.

You'd think folks would be used to things falling over by now, but no. It makes everybody tense. Like they've never seen a disaster before! So I **break the tension** with my world-famous line, "Did I do that?"

For a while I thought I needed to change the line. After all, I say it about four times a day! So I tried, "Was that done by me?" and "Is that what I did?" and "I did that, did I?" and "Did doing what I did when I did that do that to that?" But none of them sounded as good as the simple, "Did I do that?"

There are two reasons why you shouldn't use, "Did I do that?" First, because I have a certain way of saying "Did I do that?" that makes it work. Second, because it's mine. You can't have it!

But I will help you make up your own lines that will work for you in different cases. This simple exercise will get you started.

1) You've just knocked over a very expensive sculpture in your neighbor's living room. What would you say to your neighbor?
a) Hey, your sculpture thinks I'm funny. I really cracked it up!
b) That sculpture was a nice piece before. Now it's a nice *pieces*!
c) You're not losing a sculpture. You're gaining four hundred paperweights!

Now try writing your own.
d) _____!

2) You've just knocked your Laura into a pecan pie covered with whipped cream. What would you say?
a) You have the sweetest face!
b) I didn't mean to dessert you!
c) Is that a pecan on your nose or are you just glad to see me?
d) _____!

3) You spill paste all over a friend's homework. Would you say:
a) Did I glue that?
b) Good paper. Stick with it!
c) Am I making a paste of myself?
d) _____?!

You're not a bad writer! Say, if I need help writing my next book could I give you a call?
_____.

Thanks!

Foreign
Languages

English is a great language. I speak English. You speak English. Even the President speaks English.

But there are other great languages out there. And they're just waiting to be used by success seekers everywhere.

Imagine this. When your Laura passes by your locker in the morning, instead of saying, "Good morning, Laura" or "Hello there," you surprise her with "Buenos días, señorita." That's the way to say "Hello" in Spanish.

Then you look deep into her eyes and say "Allô, ma cherie!" That's the way the French say,

26

"Yo, sugar lips!" French is definitely the language of love.

Then you grab her trembling hand in yours and shout "Ti amo, amore mio!".... That's the way the Italians say "I sure am hot for you, my pet!" Italian is definitely the language of passion.

All this passion may be too much for her. She might go running off to her class. That's when you shout, "Sayonara, tekka maki!" That's the way the Japanese say "Goodbye for now, my little tuna roll!"

How to be Included
When People Forget to Invite You

Folks nowadays run around in such a hurry that they're always forgetting to invite people along. They even forget to invite people who are incredibly charming, smart, kind, witty, fun to be with, and humble like me.

When someone forgets to invite you along, **don't despair.** There are ways to get yourself invited.

Suppose someone forgets to invite you on his family camping trip. You can carefully plant the idea in his head by saying something subtle like, "I'm coming with you."

If all else fails, just show up! I know you won't find that in Emily Post's *Guide to Good Manners.* But hey. You won't find any of her rules in Steven Q. Urkel's *Guide to Success* either!

Forgetfulness isn't the only problem. Sometimes people are just too darn shy! Like my friend Carl Winslow. It seems like every time I drop in on ol' Carl he's too shy to invite me to stay. So I make it easy for him! If Carl says, "I was just having some quiet time by myself," I whisper, "Now you're having quiet time with me!"

Suppose you drop by on a shy friend and he picks up a violin and says he's in the middle of playing a solo. Just say, "Nobody should have to play a solo all by himself!" and join in with your accordion.

Kids are really shy in the cafeteria. They're too bashful to ask you to join them. So I just sit down in an empty chair next to the shy person of my choice. If she says, "My friend is sitting there," I reply, "What a nice thing to say!"

If someone's too shy to invite you to her party, make it easy for her. Call her up and say, "I hear you're having a party on Friday night." If she's still too shy to invite you, say, "I just happen to be free on Friday night." If she's *still* too shy, say, "If you don't want me to come to your party, name the capitals of the twelve smallest provinces in China." Chances are she won't say a word.

Remember, no matter how shy or forgetful people may be, **the main thing is to show up and let them see how special you are.** That way the next time they're making plans you're sure to leap into their minds!

How to
Protect Your Locker

The successful person's locker is a very important place. That's where you keep all your notebooks, your text books, your books about self-defense, your spare pair of glasses, your spare pair of suspenders, and of course, a few dozen photos of your Laura.

So **it must not be tampered with!**

To make sure no rude ruffian tries to break in, you'll definitely want some kind of protection. I myself have an ultra sensitive hi-tech alarm system that starts red lights flashing and sirens howling at the slightest touch.

Want something simpler? Train your dog to stand guard. Or make a booby trap to splatter the intruder! You could tie a bunch of spoons together with rubber bands to make a catapult that would hurl a rotten eggplant right onto his nose. Or if you don't have time to make a booby trap, you could just stand in your locker till somebody breaks in and then squash the eggplant on his nose yourself. (Don't forget to run after doing so!)

Defending Your
Honor

Honor. A simple word. A little word. A word with "on" near the beginning, and "no" near the end. A word that starts with "ho" and finishes with "or." A word that could be rearranged into "rhono," "ornoh," or "hroon."

"Hroon" means nothing. But honor means everything.

Honor is self-respect. Honor is dignity. Few words mean as much as those three consonants with a pair of "o"'s plopped in. Yes, when two "o"s are surrounded by an "n," an "r," and a silent "h" they stand for something worth fighting for.

It's all right if your nose is bloody. If it got bloody fighting for your honor, you can hold your nose up high. (As long as you hold a tissue up high, too.)

Protect your honor. Don't let anyone insult your dad. Or make fun of your mom. Or step on your pet bug. If they do, your honor has been soiled.

The best way to un-soil your honor is to get the soiler to say he's sorry.

Is fighting the best way to do this? Not really. After a fight, the honor-soiler can just walk away with his wounds. (While you crawl away with yours!) But if you attack his conscience he'll never be free.

Walk right up to him and tell him he's hurt your feelings. Sneer when he sees you. Nag when he passes. Write a note demanding an apology and photocopy it fifty times. Slide it into his locker. Mail it to his parents. Nail it to his bedroom door, his favorite wall, and his bathroom mirror. (Actually, better just tape it to the mirror.) Make it into a paper airplane and throw it at him when he's about to slurp soup or make a jump shot. **Eventually the honor-soiler is sure to say he's sorry.** He'll realize you're right, you're serious, and you're driving him insane.

One last tip: If somebody soils your honor be sure not to tell him you'll never speak to him again until he says he's sorry. This may work for some. But it takes an awfully long time to work for me!

How to Build Your Own
Laboratory
(And What to Do in it Once You've Built It)

Every successful kid needs a special place that's off limits to everybody else, where imagination can run wild: a laboratory.

To set up your laboratory, clear out some space in the basement, the garage, the tree house... even a large closet would do.

Fill the room with all kinds of junk that turns you on: gadgets, valves, tools, forks, nets, crayons, rubber bands, radios, stamps, strings, cards, cans, crates, bottles, books, paints, wires, tires, tubes, clips, cups, clays, sprays, and of course, a large photo of your Laura to inspire you.

Then, **let your mind go!** Follow the twisting, turning road of your own imagination, and see what ingenious creation you end up with.

You may end up with a heap of garbage. But you just might get lucky and end up with something incredible. Like Urkelbot!

Urkelbot is the amazing robot I came up with in my laboratory. He walks like me. He talks like me. He snorts like me. He even goes after my Laura. Urkelbot is so smart that he can even outsmart his creator! He can prevent me from turning him off. He can escape from my lab and spread terror through the neighborhood. And as he gets stronger and smarter he might even figure out how to win Laura's heart and take her away from me...

On second thought, maybe you'd be better off with a heap of garbage!

Shakespeare
and You

Don't you hate it when you can't think of the right thing to say? Wouldn't it be great to have the world's greatest writer supplying you with comeback lines? You can, if you learn a nifty trick called **"quoting Shakespeare."**

William Shakespeare was the greatest playwright who ever lived. He wrote "To be or not to be," "Wherefore art thou Romeo?," "All the world's a stage," and more. Shakespeare's got a million of 'em! His lines are so cool that grown-ups steal them all the time. Quoting Shakespeare is the one kind of stealing that makes people think more of you instead of less!

Here are a bunch of lines from Shakespeare's plays that you might want to steal. I've matched them up with some appropriate situations.

SITUATION	QUOTE
1. A big angry bully asks what your name is.	"What's in a name?"
2. Your friend wants to borrow the quarter you were saving for an ice cream sandwich.	"Neither a borrower nor a lender be."
3. You trip on the radiator in your classroom, breaking it on the coldest day of the year.	"Now is the winter of our discontent."
4. When you drop by to see your Laura she's practicing the piano.	"If music be the food of love, play on."
5. Someone tells a story about you that just isn't true.	"'Tis a tale told by an idiot."
6. When someone tries to break into your locker you squash a rotten eggplant on his nose.	"Something is rotten in the state of Denmark!"

SITUATION	**QUOTE**
7. You shout up at your Laura's window and scare her so badly that she knocks over her lamp.	"Alas, what light through yonder window breaks?"
8. Your dog Spot comes charging into your classroom.	"Out out, darn spot!"
9. While dancing at a party you split your pants right down the middle.	"Parting is such sweet sorrow."

You and Shakespeare make a good team!

I can't think how to end this chapter, so I'll steal from Shakespeare myself: "Friends, Romans, countrymen, turn the page." (That's actually a combination of Shakespeare and Urkel.)

How to Succeed in
Gym

No class is as scary as gym. Gym separates the men from the boys, the boys from the girls, and the girls from the other girls. Whether you're a man, a boy, or a girl, nobody likes being separated!

Doesn't it seem like every time you enter the gym, the teacher has set up another bunch of ropes or bars or spikes or springboards or medicine balls or pointy orange cones? **It's like walking into a torture chamber!**

But there's one simple word that will help you face all that weird, scary stuff and come out a star. This word is an important word. It's a word that takes all your time and energy. The word is a lot like honor, except that almost none of the letters are the same and they mean different things. The word, my friends, is **practice.**

It is my firm belief that you can get good at any sport with practice, practice, practice, and more practice. (And maybe even more practice after that, depending on how bad you were to begin with.)

How can you get other kids to practice a sport with you if you're terrible at it? You probably can't, but not to worry. Sports are like kissing. You can learn a lot by practicing on your own.

If you're nervous about getting hurt in gym do what I do: **Create your own sports gear for extra protection.** I've been known to strap goggles to my face, pillows to my chest, cushions to my rear, sponges to my shins, and a gigantic metal pot to the top of my head. And that was just for Ping-Pong!

On Being
Different

~~~~~~~~~~~~~~~~~~~~~~~~~~~~~~~~~~~

As you strut towards success in your own special style, people will notice. They'll stare. They'll smile. They may even laugh. In fact, they may howl with laughter and point at you and jump up and down. And why? All because you're different.

It's okay to be different. Everyone who's successful is different in some way. Rock stars are different. Sports stars are different. I'm even different. I'm so different that other people who are different call me different! Sometimes I hear people that I pass mumbling, "Hey, it's that different guy" or "Here comes Mister Different" or "Do my eyes deceive me or are we being passed by The Different-meister!" or "Why if it isn't His Royal Different-ness!"

Do not be discouraged by these dastardly despisers of difference. Don't start to hide what makes you different. Use your special gifts and skills to the fullest. That's the secret to success.

And when anyone makes fun of you for being

different just grab them by the collar, look right into their eyes, breathe on their face, and shout, "I'm no more different than Steven Q. Urkel!" That'll show them what kind of person they're dealing with!

The Importance of
the Cord Attached
to My Glasses

There are certain questions people seem to ask again and again. Questions like, "Why can't we all just live in peace?" or "How did the universe ever get started?" or "How come whenever you're nowhere near a bathroom you always need one?" But the question I hear most is, "Why do you have that incredibly long cord attached to your glasses?"

Luckily, unlike those other great questions, this one has an answer: **to keep my glasses from falling off!** A glasses' cord works like suspenders on the head. (When you think about it, the cord is also the opposite of suspenders. If the cord falls you can't see anything. If the suspenders fall everyone can see everything!)

This talk about my cord gives me an idea for a chapter about style — so turn the page for all my ideas about style. (Or don't turn the page, and spend the rest of your life wondering!)

Urkel
Style

Everybody nowadays tries so hard to keep in style. They dress like kids on TV. They wear their hair like kids in teen magazines. They're so afraid to be the least bit out of style that everybody ends up looking exactly alike. Pish tosh, people! I say, **if you want to succeed go against all the latest styles.** Here's an example that will show you why: Have you noticed that I wear my pants a tad shorter than other kids do? On a clear day you can see the tops of my white socks, and most of my shins, too! Short pant-legs have been out of style since about 1982. But I've made lots of new friends thanks to my out-of-style pants.

Everyday, somebody I don't know comes up to me to say "What happened, did they run out of material?" or "Where's the flood?" or "You look idiotic."

With witty talk like this a conversation is off and running. Soon I know a new person. And they'll never forget who I am!

Eyebrow
Power

What's the strongest part of the body? The arms? The legs? They may be able to move heavy things. But they can't move people's hearts the way my eyebrows can.

When I lean in, smile, and bounce the old brows a of couple times I become completely irresistible. As my eyebrows move up, down, and up again, they send out a message in Urkel code, saying, "You know I'm cool, don't you!"

By moving my brows in different ways I can send out other messages, like, "Please pass the mayonnaise."

If your eyebrows don't happen to be as cute and quick as mine, maybe there are other parts of your face you could use. Can you bounce your ears up and down? Or flare your nostrils? Or slide your scalp back and forth? Do you have a loose tooth you could wiggle in and out?

If you lean towards someone, smile, and start wiggling your eyebrows, nostrils, scalp, ears, and teeth, you'll send out one message loud and clear: **"I'm about as cool as Steve Urkel!"**

Quick
Wit

In the chapters on "Finding Your Own 'Did I Do That'" and "Shakespeare and You", I taught you about wit. But I neglected one key fact: Wit must be quick.

If you spill paste on somebody's paper, you can't just sit there saying "Duhh" for half an hour. You also can't walk up to the person a year later and say, "Did I glue that?" They'll think you're insane.

Slow wit is no wit! You've gotta spit out the wit on the spot. So when wit is called for, shout out the first witty thing that pops into your mind. This witty thing may not sound that witty. It might sound downright un-witty. That's why, immediately after spitting out the words of would-be wit, laugh loud!

When people hear your quick words followed by your loud laugh, they'll know they've been hit by wit.

Investing for
Success

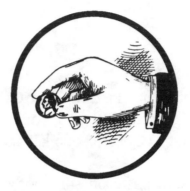

Wealth. Fortune. Riches. Can I tell you how all these can be yours? No. But I can tell you how to make a few bucks by investing.

Investing means putting money in a special place. Is the counter at your favorite candy shop a special place? Nice try. To invest, you have to put your money somewhere it can make more money.

I've got money in a savings account, a mutual fund, a CD (Certification of Deposit), an IRA (Interest Retirement Account), and a **FASYMUYTTYPA** (Forget About Seeing Your Money Until You're Three Times Your Present Age).

In each of these accounts my money makes more money every day. For every month I keep

$10 in a savings account it makes .475¢ (almost a nickel)!

Almost a nickel may not sound like much. But that's about the cost of a piece of bubble gum! That's about the cost of the buckle on a suspender! That's about the cost of the first forty-five seconds of a movie!

My money's working for me, which is a lot easier than me working for it. But before your money can start working for you, you've got to come up with some money to invest. Here are ten ways to raise money for your first investment.

1. **Play a musical instrument in a public place.** (When I play my accordion in the park everybody throws coins — along with whatever else happens to be within reach.)

2. **Write love poems for other people's Lauras.** (Charge different prices so everybody can afford one: $2 for a poem on pink stationery, $1 for loose-leaf, 25¢ for a napkin.)

3. **Set up a stand that sells ice cold lemonade.** (This might not be such a good idea in Alaska.)

4. **Set up a stand that sells hot chocolate.** (This might not be such a good idea in Miami Beach.)

5. **Offer to help out your parents around the house.** (My father once gave me $5 to help him put a piece of masking tape on my mouth.)

6. **Offer to mow your neighbor's lawn.** (Remember to *cut the grass only*; steer clear of roses, azaleas, and poodles.)

7. **Tutor other kids in math.** (If *you're* terrible at math be sure to hire someone to tutor *you* first.)

8. **Work extra hours at your job.** (Bosses really like workers who'll stay late on Saturday nights — though they get upset when they find you asleep on the job.)

9. **Rent out space in your locker.** (Let kids who can't fit something in their lockers leave it in yours for the day — the bigger the item the more you charge. Maybe 50¢ for an ice skate, 75¢ for a saxophone, $1 for a baboon.)

10. **Lend out your copy of this book.** (For a book jammed with tips this hot you should be able to charge at least $5 — an hour!)

Getting the Teacher
to Call on You

Nothing's more frustrating than knowing the answer to a question and being unable to say it. So I've written this little poem that tells how to get the teacher to call on you.

"Ode to Getting Called On"
by Steven Q. Urkel

When you've got smart stuff to say
Shoot your hand up right away
Groan and moan and gasp for air
Till you're sure she sees it there

Keep on reaching way up high
Yelp like you're about to die
Grunt and sigh and keep on trying
Switch arms if the first is dying

When at last she calls on you
As she'll finally have to do
Say the thing that's on your mind
Then collapse, if so inclined!

Writing the
Love Poem

As I just showed, poetry can be pretty powerful.
But no poem packs more power on the page than
the poem of pure personal passion. (Try
saying that out loud without spitting on the book!)

Here's a love poem for your Laura. Read it to
her and it's sure to tickle her ear. Just fill in the
blanks.

"How Do I Love Thee?"

by Steven Q. Urkel and _____ __. _____
                                    (Your Name)
How do I love thee?
Since you asked, I'll tell
I love you when you're _____ing
Which you do extremely well

I love your dandy _____
And your _____ clothes
I love you when you're _____
Or _____ your nose

I love you every _____
And every _____ too
Yes, even when you're _____
Which even you must do!

I love you more than _____
or _____ that tastes so sweet
I even love the _____
Which _____ upon your feet!

So even though I _____
and _____ now and then
You must admit I'm _____
With a paper and a pen!

Farewell

Alas, faithful reader, the time has come for this book to come to an end. I must pass the torch to a new generation of Urkels. I must set you free to climb every mountain and cross every stream. I must stop typing before my fingers fall off. As I look back over all these pages, four words spring to mind. No, not "Did I do that?" The words are, **"Reach for the stars."** If you set your sights high and reach with everything you've got, you're bound for success.

Of course, you might not be able to pluck down every single star you ever wanted. But you won't get any if you don't reach!

Sayonara !

P.S. There's a quick quiz coming up to see if you've been paying attention.

Urk-Zam

1. To win someone's heart you should:
   a) smother the person with kindness
   b) smother the person with meanness
   c) smother the person with onions

2. To hold your pants up you need:
   a) a box of paper clips
   b) a roll of Scotch tape
   c) a pair of suspenders

3. To succeed at your job you should:
   a) just do what you can
   b) just do more than you can
   c) just do the cancan

4. To succeed at hand-to-hand combat you should:
   a) study and move quickly
   b) listen to records and move slowly
   c) eat a lot and move to Canada

5. To succeed on the dance floor you've got to be:
   a) crazy
   b) smelly
   c) yourself

6. When breaking into song you might try using someone else's:
   a) voice
   b) clothes
   c) tune

7. The key to the kiss is the:
   a) the lighting
   b) the pucker
   c) the apology

8. Your _____ should set you apart.
   a) number of heads
   b) laugh
   c) local police officer

9. Once you've chosen your laugh you should:
   a) be brave
   b) be ashamed
   c) begin choosing your cry

10. Steven Urkel has been incredibly cool ever since the day he was:
   a) awarded a prize for his science experiment
   b) kissed by Laura
   c) born

11. When you find yourself standing among a bunch of furniture that has somehow tumbled to the ground you should:
    a) say nothing
    b) say something
    c) change schools

12. To surprise your true love, you might try wishing her "good morning" in:
    a) a foreign language
    b) a foreign accent
    c) the evening

13. If people forget to invite you, you can always just:
    a) show up
    b) shut up
    c) blow up

14. You might try using a few spoons, a rubber band, and a rotten eggplant to protect your:
    a) planet
    b) country
    c) locker

15. Never let anyone soil your:
    a) carpet
    b) honor
    c) soil

16. You should let your imagination run wild in your:
    a) laboratory
    b) dentist's office
    c) principal's office

17. "To be or not to be" was written by
    a) a bee
    b) William Shakespeare
    c) a two-year-old child

18. Improving at sports takes _____, _____, and more _____.
    a) watching tv, napping, watching TV
    b) ice cream, candy, ice cream
    c) practice, practice, practice

19. It's okay to be:
    a) rude
    b) different
    c) looking at the paper of the person next to you

20. Most people are too concerned with dressing in:
    a) style
    b) clothes
    c) front of a crowd

21. Putting money aside where it can make money is:
    a) impossible
    b) illegal
    c) investing

22. You can use parts of your face to:
    a) pull a tree up by the roots
    b) scratch your back
    c) send out a message that you're cool

23. A witty remark is only funny if you say it:
    a) right away
    b) softly to yourself a year later
    c) while wearing a chicken suit

24. To get the teacher to call on you:
    a) raise your hand and sigh
    b) raise your ham on rye
    c) raisin bran and pie

Correct Answers:

1) A 2) C 3) B 4) A 5) C 6) C 7) B 8) B
9) A 10) C 11) B 12) A 13) A 14) C 15) B
16) A 17) B 18) C 19) B 20) A 21) C
22) C 23) A 24) A

So how'd you do?

Correct Answers	Evaluation
1-2	Not very good
3-4	Not very bad
5-6	Not bad
7-8	Almost good
9-10	Pretty good
11-12	Pretty darn good
13-14	Very good
15-16	Extremely good
17-18	Incredibly good
19-21	Amazingly good
22	Pretty great
23	Extremely incredibly *amazingly* great
24	Urkel